How to Create a Profitable Marketing Strategy for Your Law Firm

By Noah Carmichael

https://insideexecutive247.com

Contents

Chapter 5: Building Your Online Reputation

Chapter 6: Call Tracking and Conversation Analytics

Chapter 7: Creating Closed-Loop Analytics to Improve Conversions

Appendix

Introduction

No one **WANTS** to talk to you.

If you are an attorney, you should know exactly what I mean by that statement. The services and guidance you provide on a daily basis are not the same as going to a flower shop or getting a cell phone fixed.

Your potential clients are not always coming to you in the best of situations. It can be a sobering experience to finally commit to getting assistance from a lawyer. Knowing this is the case then, why would you market yourself and your law firm in the same manner as a flower shop or cell phone repair store? Your advice and guidance are considerably more valuable than getting flowers or a new iPhone screen.

Your audience is unique in their approach in choosing to hire your firm for services. They utilize different devices; they are more apt to think, and rethink, and overthink their choice of the right attorney for them. They may ask for referrals from friends and family, look you up online and check your reviews, take a quick look at your website, look up your bar information, etc. You see, their path to a decision will differ from the guy looking for flowers for his wife, or the dad looking to fix his son's cell phone…again.

While performing marketing for different industries over the years, there seems to be a mindset that what is good for every other industry is also going to work for law firms. In my experience, that is not true.

Are there similarities, yes.

Are there lessons to be learned from other industries, yes.

Should your law firm marketing strategy mirror a cell phone repair company? Not at all.
I am not going to disparage the flower shop owner or say that the cell phone repair owner is not as trained or as smart as you the attorney. I will say that your specialized training makes you different.

Think about this for a second. You can be intimidating. You should be intimidating. You are a highly trained professional that has sacrificed time, energy, and money into becoming who you are today. You should be compensated handsomely for it. Why do you think your client's purchasing journey differs from any other industry?

You are a big-ticket item. If you are fortunate enough to be chosen by your clients, their expectations far exceed anything they may have been looking for in flower or cell phone repair shop. Your fee will also far exceed the cost of a flower or a cell phone. They know this going into a conversation with you, and your marketing strategy must match who you are and what you bring to the table as a firm from marketing to the first engagement with your front desk, to signing on the dotted line as a client.

So let's go back to my first statement. No one WANTS to talk to you…and it is not about you moreover, it is about them. They NEED to talk to you.

Your potential clients are asking these questions:
- How will divorce impact my children?
- How will this DUI impact my job?
- Can I get just probation on my criminal charges?
- Should I file bankruptcy?
- Do I have a claim for this slip and fall?

If it is about them, then you must make your marketing talk to your potential clients when they want it, where they want it, and most importantly, when they NEED it. Look at those five questions again.

Do you think the message and timing of those messages will differ depending on your firm's specialty? I would hope your answer is yes. Now, look at your current marketing strategy. Do you know the time window for your DUI messaging? Are you aware of the time of day your potential clients may be searching for divorce information?

Let's go back to the flower shop and cell phone repair shop again. Do you think their potential customers are looking for their services at 3 a.m.? They could be, sure, but I doubt not having flowers is keeping them up at night.

Now, look at what you offer.

Having been through a divorce and, sadly, knowing people that have gone through a divorce, there were times that I might have been on my cell phone at 3 a.m. looking for answers to my questions. Would your firm have put that information in front of me when I needed it the most? Would that information have talked about you or talked to my questions at 3 a.m.?

It is naïve to think that your potential clients are only looking for you during typical office hours. So why would you follow that cookie-cutter marketing plan for a local mom and pop retail shop? Your services and value are different, your clients are different, and your marketing strategy should be different from any other profession in your local community.

This means that your firm must take a client-centered, data-driven approach to marketing.

Gone are the days when just PPC or just SEO will do the trick. Gone is the fly by night email marketing newsletter that was a "waste of money" because your goals were not clear. PPC, SEO,

Email marketing, Social Media marketing and brand reach must match and pull towards the one common goal of your firm.

That goal?

To secure new business consistently and be the ONLY firm of choice in your vertical(s) when your potential clients need you the most. When potential clients look up your services, the quality of your work and your firm's reputation should show from your marketing message, leading to your website, and then the first impression upon contact with your firm.

Your entire marketing plan should work hand-in-hand. Your offline presence is just as important as your online presence. Traditional marketing still works in today's market if done correctly. This is why we call it a marketing strategy. Attorneys are one of those professions where traditional marketing still needs to be integrated into your entire plan. Does that mean you have to break your budget? Not at all. It's called a budget, so figure out how to work within it.

An online presence is an important aspect of your law firm's growth and development. Search engines are where new prospective clients will find you, but there are many reasons why online marketing can help boost your practice, and search is just one part of the bigger picture. There are more than 131 billion online searches every month, ignoring your potential to be seen online represents a huge opportunity cost.

Word of mouth and referral traffic is also a powerful marketing tool in law, but you cannot solely rely on referrals. Do you know how many people find themselves in a panic and searching vehemently online for a local attorney to save the day? That hero could be you! Adopting relevant internet marketing strategies will help differentiate your law firm from competitors, show prospective clients that you are technologically savvy, and most importantly present all the necessary tools your clients need.

Not surprisingly, your aim should not be to push your law firm or being "salesy" at all. Being pushy about your practice can and will turn off prospective clients. Instead, you want to position your law firm as the expert firm in your area of practice. This will be accomplished by publishing client-centered content that would be helpful as a resource to your target audience. Being a relevant source of information to your potential clients will allow you to accomplish several things:

1. To potential clients, you stand out as legal experts in a given field. When they are eventually in need of your services; your law firm will be top of mind.

2. Posting and publishing content online also increases your search engine rankings, meaning it is easier to be found when those potential clients search for firms like yours.

3. Quality client-centered content will help you position your firm as an expert within your community, in your professional associations, and for the media.

4. Showing up in search results will give you additional name recognition and credibility.

In this book, we will discuss a client-centered marketing strategy for your law firm. Every chapter will discuss different marketing strategies, both online and offline, to help you build your presence. At the end of each chapter, you will also find a section titled, **"Where Do I Start."** These sections will provide some guidance and quick tips for you to implement in your marketing immediately.

As a bonus, you will also receive two checklists. The first checklist will cover some of the items mentioned in the book that will help you stay on track. The second checklist will be for those looking to hire a marketing strategy firm. The questions in this final checklist will help you and your staff make a more informed decision on hiring the right legal marketing consultant.

Chapter 1: The Client-Centered Website Design

Most law firm websites are focused on one aspect – promoting their firm and its lawyers. In this chapter, we will discuss a different approach to law firm website development: The Client-Centered Web Design.

A client-centered web design is based on one theme- answering the question - "How will the firm serve me?" With a client-centered web design, every aspect of the website, including attorney profiles and practice areas, is centered on how the firm serves clients.

Rather than focusing on quantitative lists of great legal achievements of the firm and its lawyers, a client-centered website design aims to create and develop a relationship with potential clients around how the needs of the client will be served by the firm. The achievement of the law firm and attorneys are carefully present in a way that shows value to be provided to the clients, not as a tribute to the firm or its attorneys.

4 Critical Aspects of a Good Client-Centered Web Design

1. **Have a Good Client Service Statement**
   A good client-centered website will be focused on sending a specific message that shows how the firm serves its customers. This is what is known as a **client-service statement**.

An effective client-service statement should not be detailed or overly-complicated. The client-service statement should also not be a core values statement or a mission statement. Remember that a core values statements focus on central beliefs of the firm, while a mission statement focuses on the organization's reason for existence. While either a core values statement or a mission statement might concern clients, clients do not necessarily need to be included.

Here is a client service statement example for a family law firm:

> **"We *provide pro-active legal counsel, assisting our clients in understanding how the laws of (Your state) impact their families. We will successfully represent our clients in litigations, negotiations, financing and other crucial matters as they arise.*"**

2. **Concentrate on User Experience or UX**

User Experience here refers to website essentials, such as navigational aids being easily noticeable and identifiable by your prospective clients. These navigational aids them to quickly figure out what they can expect by visiting your website. Therefore, UX is essential in assisting users to predict their needs and reasons for viewing your website.

No matter what page of the site a user goes to, he will always be able to find his way back to another section, since the navigation bar is ever-present and grabs their attention. This creates a feeling of order and confidence to your prospective clients. Remember that a guideline to use is to be 3-clicks away at all times.

3. **Make Accessibility and Site Orientation a Priority**

   Your prospective clients will want to find the information they are looking for quickly and efficiently. Accessibility can thus take shape and form of any number of things, from a basic search feature to a sitemap page. Other ideas may include organizing web content into sections that can be digested easily by utilizing a format that is reasonable to the users and even making it effortless for the users to skim your texts.

   Site Orientation, on the other hand, can be achieved by using navigational clues that can include descriptive links, sitemap and highly visible site elements on each page that tell the user where they are relative to other pages, as well as how to navigate to different pages.

4. **Tie Together a Good Visual Design**

   Visual design refers to the aesthetics of your entire interface. Your visual design takes the center stage in communicating both tone and information to your prospective clients. Some of the important features of a good visual design include web pages that feature a mix of being interesting, yet simple, with a conservative use of colors that make the most vital elements the most visually prominent.

To maximize the effectiveness of a firm's message, color combinations, creative arts and images should be used. More importantly, your homepage should not be filled with awards that the firm or attorneys have recently won, unless these aspects are presented as a benefit to your prospective clients.

At the same time, remember that you are a law firm and not an ice cream shop. Research color schemes in marketing and how they make an impact on the psychological side of marketing to potential clients.

Client-Centered Website Design Should Not be an After-Thought

Some web designers forget the whole point of their trade: Ensuring the site is user-centered. When that happens, you get a site that will frustrate users and end up being nothing more than a hard slog through which to navigate. Yes, there are numerous aspects of a client-centered design on which to focus. However, an experienced and skilled web designer will ensure that all of them are addressed appropriately.

Good design is a process from start to finish, one that should not be rushed and requires a good deal of thoughts and consideration. Your clients are everything; thus it stands to reason that you should design your site in a way it makes their experience as delightful as you possibly can.

Where Do I Start?

If you are starting your site from scratch, there are a few items you have to familiarize yourself with. I am going to be captain obvious here and first suggest that you purchase a web domain. No, we are not going to go through step-by-step on how to do this here, but here is a bit of advice.

Pick a domain name that fits your law firm and brand. In the past, webmasters suggested that you pick a web domain that mirrors the keyword you want to rank for. If you are purchasing a brand new site, stay away from this tactic. Google will **NOT** penalize you for picking this type of web domain; however, they have provided guidance, as of October 2017, that identifies this "hack" as outdated.

Next, find a web host for your new WordPress website. Yes, you can get a site from anywhere nowadays, but here is the rub. You may see the commercials that advertise the fact that you can just put up a site online. Those are 100% accurate. You can just put up a site online, but then what?

Having a site built on a WordPress platform allows you more flexibility for now and in the future. With that said, make sure you shop around. There are cheap packages and expensive packages available but as the adage goes, "You get what you pay for."

I have personally taken over client sites from web hosting companies that I have never heard of. What makes it worse, is that when you look to migrate over to a reputable option, there is no customer service and the website owner (you) have a vague idea of what you purchased. This is your property, and it should be treated as such.

Your next step is to look into taking a few tutorials from WordPress Beginner. Side note here, I am not affiliated nor do I generate any income by referring you to WordPress Beginner. Having done this for a while, I follow other industry blogs, and if I were to start my website from scratch, I would use their tutorials as a tool. If you are starting from scratch, I recommend you do the same.

Bottom line is that you are going to have to do a little research. Here are a few providers to get you started:

- Bluehost.com
- Godaddy.com
- Wordpress.org
- Wordpress.com

There is low cost, and then there is cheap, know the difference. Your law firm website is a long-term investment, and your hands should be all over it from the beginning.

Chapter 2: Content Strategy and Development

Content Strategy: A Development Guide

Content is no longer an optional part of a law firm's marketing strategy. Gone are the days when posting an article stuffed with target keywords could boost a page's search ranking. Now, poor quality content has a far more negative impact on a site. Thus, focus on producing quality content, and you will increase your SERP rankings and User Experience. The key is creating good content that answers your potential client's questions while still positioning your firm as the go-to firm for their legal issues.

However, how can you come up with a sound content strategy? If you want to drive organic traffic to your site, what exact strategies should you use to build the right amount of organic traffic? In this chapter, we will explain the process of creating a content strategy and discuss proven content marketing methods that drive traffic.

What Exactly is Content Strategy?

Content strategy is the planning, development, management, and distribution of content across multiple channels. A solid content strategy is a key to delivering a compelling user experience for your law firm. Once you start producing great content and engage your users with it and boost rankings at the same time.

Developing a sound content strategy is not as difficult as it sounds. The tips below will help you.

Tip 1: Define Your Goals

Great content is created for a great purpose, and this purpose must be defined. Before creating content, ask yourself how you want to improve search ranking results, attract future clients, convert users, generate leads for a book or boost firm awareness. After determining your goals, you need to determine how your content strategy will assist you.

For instance, if you want to boost law firm awareness, you can use whitepaper, eBook, Tip sheet, Checklists, How to Video or an Educational Webinar. Similarly, if you want to help clients evaluate your firm, you can use a webinar, case study, Data Sheet, FAQ or a Demo Video.

As a law firm, I would suggest that your number one goal is generating inbound phone calls for your practice. Downloads and views are nice but a ringing phone keeps your law firm open.

Tip 2: Know Your Audience

To create an effective content strategy, you must know your audience. You can get this information by finding out what kind of sites your potential clients are visiting, the content they like engaging with as well as which social media sites they like sharing their content on.

If you already have a functional website, you can do this by enabling Google Analytics. Google Analytics can help you determine what type of content your clients are interested in. With this information, create information that is targeted to the user rather than content you want to read. Your aim should be to create content that will help you increase Page Views, decrease Bounce Rate, and increase Average Time on Page.

Within your Google Analytics Account, you will be able to set up goals. Make sure that one of those goals focuses on inbound phone calls. When consulting clients, we do look at views and bounce rates, but ultimately, the job of your marketing is to convert those views into appointments. Use the views and bounce rates to guide you along your sales funnel as leading indicators of your overall reach.

Tip 3: Provide Valuable Content
The internet is full of content that should not even exist. This content does not provide any real value. 99 percent of internet users do not find this useless content since it does not appear anywhere near the top of SERPs. To ensure your content is always found, make sure you create content that stands out. Good content should be 100 percent original, have a distinctive voice and offer great value to your target readers. This way you will establish yourself as an authority in your field.

I cannot overstate the originality of your content. Your value will not be restating the letter of the law. The real value will come in the "voice" you present and have for your clients' interests. Just as in law school, feel free to reference cases or journals with the appropriate credits given. Keep in mind, however, that unlike law school, the end user does not need to hear your legal jargon. The need to hear your compassion, your focus and maybe even a taste of your general strategy for assisting them.

Write content based on the latest news and how it may impact a client's decision making in a particular area. Here is an example. If you are an immigration attorney and are not taking advantage of the immigration news cycle of the past few years, you are missing a golden opportunity to write heartfelt, socially impactful content.

Tell stories of past clients but make them more than just case studies. Make them stories that potential clients can relate to. A story that makes anyone that visits your website or social media hit the share button. Provide real value.

Tip 4: Measure Your Results
This is one of the most important aspects of developing an effective content strategy. Measuring your results of content marketing efforts allows you to determine what your target audience likes and what they do not like and reasons behind it. A good tool for measuring your content marketing results is again,

Google Analytics. It shows you the number of times a page was viewed, bounce rate and the average time on page.

Take a moment to view Google's YouTube videos to learn the basics. Your priority is to be a lawyer; I get it. You are also running a business. Know enough of the basics to ask questions of marketers that you may hire some day.

What Types of Content Should You Create?

Content is the heart of most successful internet marketing or SEO campaigns. Your content should help your potential clients solve their problems, by providing the information they are looking for. Remember the client-centered website? The same goes for content. For example, if your law firm handles criminal cases, the content on your site should provide answers to various sections of Criminal law. To an individual charged with DUI, your site should provide solutions to their questions. To take this a step further, your content should also show up when they need it the most.

Similarly, you can create content that aims to educate readers about your areas of expertise. Creating Criminal law-related content that educates your customers and boosts your credibility as a Law Firm that specializes in criminal cases. Who will read this, past clients, prospective clients looking for advice from a criminal attorney?

Remember, don't be afraid to tell a story. The story could be your philosophy or reasoning to take on specific criminal cases. Let's say that you have a family member that used to be a gang member in the Los Angeles area and for whatever reason; you attract those clients by word of mouth.

Guess what? Those types of clients are using computers also. So are their family members. Why can't your content tell the story of why defending them is important to you? Why can't your content speak to some of the cases you have assisted your clients with and what those cases mean to you personally?

Do not forget the story. Has one of your past clients turned their life around based on a strategy you used some years back as a public defender or when you first opened your practice? Why not create a piece of Q&A content written with that client in the form of an interview? How would that look you ask?

Ask that client to answer 5-10 questions about how your strategy assisted them from beginning to end:

- How the client felt before meeting you?
- How did they feel about your process and strategy during the duration of their case?
- What have they gone on to do with their life since your assistance?
- How did your assistance impact their family?

You could do that with Family Law, Immigration, DUI, and other fields of law. Get creative and think outside of the box. These are the types of stories that resonate and connect with people. As you will see in the coming sections, you can also repurpose this content in different mediums across multiple platforms and best of all, it is evergreen. This type of content can live on your website or social properties forever.

Branded Content

Branded Content refers to any content that can be associated with your law firm. This is the kind of content that makes a prospective client think of your firm by name. In these recent times, top publishers such as NYT and Buzzfeed use branded content to boost revenue on their sites and on social channels, while keeping their readers intrigued. Great branded content can come in various forms, but share these three characteristics:

1) Your content should match the tone of your audience. Talk with them, not at them.

2) It sells your "concept" not your services: It focuses on the story and execution of that story rather than selling the services of your firm.

3) It Entertains: It engages and draws the reader or view immediately with emotions and storytelling.

The principles of good branded are value, relevancy, and quality. Branded content relies the delicate balance of creating client-centered stories and tying that information into your firms messaging or brand. If your content is interesting, compelling, and entertaining, then it will deliver good results. Let's look at four types of branded-content we can use:

1) **Videos**

    It is no secret that the use of video in content marketing is on the rise. Video has been proven to demand more consumer attention than any other medium. Research shows that an average user spends 88 percent of their time on websites with video. Like regular content marketing, video content marketing is a strategic marketing approach that should put the needs and wants of your clients first.

    Video marketing may seem confusing or just jump out initially as too much. But you may already have your video content sitting in front of you. It is called old blog posts. This should be your starting point. Take some old blog posts and repurpose them into videos. Please, whatever you do, let's stay away from reading them verbatim off of a piece of paper. I only say this because I have seen it.

    One of the objections I hear often is cost. While this is a fair point, technology has made it possible to record your initial videos on your iPhone. I have consulted clients with low budgets to give it a try. Sit in front of your desk in your office, set up your phone on a tripod and start talking. You may be surprised that some of your videos will come out with exceptional quality. When you are able to increase your budget, look at hiring a professional, but do not make the excuse that you do not have the tools to at least get started.

2) **Whitepapers**

Did you know that whitepapers were the most preferred content type used to make purchase decisions in the last 12 months? Additionally, whitepapers, webinars, and eBooks were the top three last year, when it came to most valued content types. Clients are more likely to share whitepaper content with their colleagues.

Whitepapers can help you build trust, credibility and thought leader status. To be successful, your whitepaper marketing must capture and keep the attention and interest of your readers. It must make them want to make the next step in the buying process, which is hiring your legal team.

Will white papers work with all types of law? The answer is no, but if you practice Intellectual Property Law, Securities Law, or Business Litigation, whitepapers may very well set you apart by providing your potential clients something substantive that they can attach to your law firm.

3) **Case Studies**

Marketing is all about sharing services to your prospective clients, and case studies are a great way of accomplishing this. A case study is an in-depth analysis that tells a story about a client and your law firm. In fact, 92 percent of clients prefer that media messages sound like a story. Think of a case study as an expansion of your client's testimonials.

Despite the name, the case study is a pretty straightforward concept that yields numerous benefits for your law firm whether you are marketing to consumers or business-to-business.

These case studies can be easily exchanged for email addresses for those not ready to commit just yet. You can also add case studies to your website to show not only your wealth of knowledge but improve your SEO and PPC campaigns. Google and other search engines are leaning away from keyword focused content and providing more power to those pieces of content that are helping clients solve problems. Case studies do just that.

4) **Podcasts**

Podcasts are an important aspect of content marketing yet are underused in the legal profession. Podcasting provides a passive means for the listener to digest content. Podcasts are very personal. When someone hears you speak, he or she is able to hear your authenticity and personality. This makes it easy for them to meet, like and trust you. Podcasts help your prospective clients to feel as if they already know you on individual level.

There really are no rules for how long your podcast should be. What if you made your podcast 5 minutes per week and titled it, "5 Minutes with (insert your first name)." Your format could be that you answer an uncommon question that you are hearing from your current clients in Family Law.

Just like your videos, you can not only use this podcast on your website, but also create the expectation on your social media that your podcast comes out every Thursday at noon. Are you telling me you do not have 5 minutes per week for your audience or potential clients to get to know you?

A podcast could also be an alternative to those too shy to get in front of the camera.

In these recent times, it is more challenging than ever to differentiate your law firm's brand. Having a sound content marketing strategy can help you plug your firm directly into the conversation by providing information your target audience wants. When used effectively, content marketing can help you increase long-term visibility and deliver real business results.

Where Do I Start?

The first place to start is by clearly defining your audience. This is going to be a necessary step because not everyone is a client. In knowing that, we do not want to waste our content efforts on those that are less likely to hire your firm.

Let's say that you are an Intellectual Property Attorney. It is time to set up shop on LinkedIn in addition to your blog. The reasoning here is that your audience is here already. It is fairly easy to tie these two platforms together to work in your favor.

Here is how this could work for your firm.

Every time you go to a networking event or Chamber of Commerce meeting, you should be exchanging contact information with fellow business owners. Ask them if it is okay to connect on LinkedIn as well. Set up your profile to direct your followers to your blog posts, whether it be video, case studies, or your weekly posts. How would you do this?

LinkedIn Pulse is the answer. Pulse allows you to leverage their LinkedIn audience and the connections you have built to share your content and put in front of like-minded individuals. Once there on your Pulse blog, direct readers to your blog for more content. This builds trust with your audience and potential clients. Putting your content on Pulse will also build trust and reinforce your position as a thought leader.

The same can be done with Instagram, Twitter, Facebook, Medium, BeBee, and others. It depends on where your audience is engaging.

Chapter 3: Traditional Marketing and Building Offline Authority

If you are reading this chapter, then you probably already know the growing importance of digital media in the law firm marketing world. Unfortunately, many law firms think that investing in internet marketing methods means abandoning the proven traditional marketing techniques behind.

Using traditional marketing to supplement your online marketing techniques is an effective method of marketing and far more useful than using either on its own. Traditional marketing techniques, such as mailings, billboards, print collateral, and television ads all have historically high success rates. Depending on whom you take advice from, the success rates of these mediums have been decreasing. I am not in that boat. I firmly believe that a solution is to use a combination of both internet and traditional marketing techniques together.

Think of it this way. Do you want all of your eggs in one basket? I would think not. When giving a consultation, this is one of the areas I look at during a competitive analysis. Being a lawyer, you already know that your field is highly competitive. If you are not there, your competition very well may be there. If it is not in your budget now, start planning it now and be prepared once you can comfortably integrate some traditional marketing channels into your overall marketing campaign.

In this Chapter, we will review a few traditional marketing methods that still work today and discuss ways you can supplement these techniques with your overall marketing strategy.

5 Traditional Marketing Methods That Still Work

1. **Business Cards**

   Business cards are used by business owners to introduce themselves to others in a sophisticated manner. This form of traditional marketing is still used today to promote businesses. You need to keep your business card in your pocket so that you suitably present it to all types of clients. Business cards also help you to create a connection with your client, which is very essential.

   Do not forget that your card has two sides. Have a QR code or your website or both on the back and present your business cards in that way if you are physically handing your card to someone. Point out that your website is on the back if they want more information about your firm and what stories you are telling on your website.

   Some people are old school in that way. Remember also that there are apps that can scan your business card and automatically connect me to your LinkedIn or other social media profiles.

2. **Direct Marketing**

Brochures and flyers were historically used to come into direct contact with local customers as well as business clients. Leaving a nice flyer or brochures with businesses or people you think could be interested in your services was considered to be enough at that time. Today, law firms can still use this method to offer special gifts to get the attention of first-time clients. This traditional marketing technique still contains that special personal touch that, depending on the services the client is seeking.

Hand out your brochures or flyers after your consultation. Again, have your online properties listed and point them out to prospective clients. Trade brochures with local business owners in your immediate area.

3. **Word of Mouth/Referral**
   This is one the essential traditional marketing techniques used by businesses and is still a required source for firms. Today, law firms can still organize charitable events along with their online content to receive promotion via word of mouth.

   I am not a proponent of showing up to every event available, so choose them wisely. If you assist business owners with company formation documentation or acting as general counsel, I do hope you are showing up to your local chamber of commerce meetings or mixers.

One word of advice about networking. Do not be "that guy" at the networking event. If you have ever been to one, you know what I mean. The guy that comes off as "qualifying me" as a lead from hello. We have all run across that at some point. Yes, I understand that your run a business and clients are what keeps you open, but there are other ways to do it.

Here is an example of what I mean. Some years ago, I went to a networking event in Scottsdale. The event brings in a few thousand people annually from all over Arizona in various industries. I sit down next to a gentleman, and he starts qualifying me immediately before the start of the seminar we were both attending.

Within a few quick minutes, he qualified me a potential lead for a life insurance product and may also be able to help me with my 401k. Sounds great for him right? When he finally asks me what I did for a living, I mentioned that I was a Financial Advisor and I happen to manage 401k's and group life insurance policies for a few companies in town.

The look on his face and the ear-to-ear smile on mine was priceless. It gets better. The seminar we were at you ask?

"How **Not** to Do Networking." When the "don't qualify everyone you meet here" section came up, all we both could do was laugh.

I have left Finance for some years now, but guess who I will not be calling if I need someone to assist me with my retirement or asset protection. That guy.

Get to know people and create a network of fellow professionals that see you as "their guy" when it comes time to get legal advice.

4. **Warm Calls**

   If you know a client that is potentially interested in your legal services, then a warm call can be an ideal way of contacting clients to introduce yourself. You can also send an email to establish or reestablish the connection. This can serve as the initial step for your face-to-face meeting with them.

   Warm calls can be generated from your case studies, webinars, podcasts, or whitepapers. This will obviously not work for every field in law but it still works.

5. **Press Releases**

   Press Releases are published by businesses to introduce new products or services in the market or to announce the addition of new features to existing products or services. In today's law firm marketing, this traditional marketing method can be used when introducing new legal services, partnerships, and updates to your prospective clients and surrounding community.

Don't forget that you can also use press releases to showcase new team members. Maybe there was a highly sought after paralegal or attorney in your area with a reputation that follows them to whichever firm they are with. Wouldn't you want that to be known? Use the press release to introduce them and how they fit into your client-centered culture.

At first glance, you may doubt the effectiveness of these traditional marketing techniques. Keep in mind; these examples are just a few examples of TOMA or Top of Mind Awareness. Combining these traditional marketing efforts with your digital strategy will pay off if done correctly.

How to Keep Your Law Firm "Top of Mind"

When an incident arises that you can solve, you want your law firm to be the first firm your client thinks about. You want to be the leader in your niche, the go-to-lawyer, a trusted name in the legal field. In other words, you want your brand to be the Top of Mind. A good law firm should be able to communicate its values, mission, and vision well.

However, without a good Top of Mind marketing strategy, your firm will fail to be the go-to you want it to be. So how can you make your firm the first name that comes to the mind of your prospective clients? Let's look at five quick tips:

1) **Make an Emotional Connection:** Emotional satisfaction is taken into account whenever a client determines the net benefit of hiring your firm. Determining the emotional connection of your clients allows you to know how to approach them before they hire your firm.

2) **Always be Present**: Rarely will clients hire your firm after learning about it for the first time. It is important to always to know where your prospective client is regarding platform. Craft your strategy to be there on a regular basis.

3) **Offer Value Consistently:** Prospective clients should all feel your value when they interact with your law firm. Having a regular blog that contains valuable information for your clients is the best way to accomplish this. You can always tie in your traditional marketing efforts to point back to a central location online.

4) **Be Unique:** Achieve Top of Mind status by being one of the law firms that is different from the rest. Some of the ideas presented earlier in the book may work for you. I would advise you to see what your competitors are doing.

They may have some good ideas, or you may be able to take over an area they neglected.

5) **Create a Buzz:** Marketing at its core is about getting attention. One of the best ways of doing this is by getting people to talk about your firm. Determine what will make your target audience recommend your brand to their family and friends. Don't forget to utilize your staff as well. If you are truly in this together, give your staff some ownership in creating ideas that will create a buzz within your community. Volunteer for park clean ups, food drives, helping veterans and more.

If follow these five tips, you will certainly make your law firm achieve a Top of Mind status. Now that you know how Top of Mind marketing works let's learn how you can use it to supplement your online marketing.

Using Traditional Marketing to Supplement Digital Marketing

Integration of your traditional and digital marketing efforts are going to allow your firm to cast a wider net from which to attract potential clients. Do not overlook silver spenders who are mostly digital immigrants accustomed to traditional marketing. Remember, we are now in an era where life expectancy is longer. You have Baby Boomers, Generation X, Millennials, and coming to a market near you, Generation Z.

Each generation has their preferred method of contact, but one thing is common. The need for a competent and trustworthy attorney. If can integrate your marketing efforts and talk to each audience on their preferred platform, you will have a higher chance of success.

Here are three ways that the two approaches can be integrated to enhance the impact of your marketing efforts.

1) **Passive and Active**

   Traditional marketing is considered passive, while online marketing is considered active. This means both methods can complement each other to achieve your set goals and objectives.

2) **Numerous Channels**

   Using digital and traditional marketing methods enable your firm's message to be spread across multiple channels efficiently. Depending on your target audience, some media platforms work better than others. Although everyone is exposed to different kinds of media, your younger audience is likely to be more digital. By utilizing both methods, your law firm will be able to reach a large number of potential customers.

If you are using social media channels currently, get into your analytics and see what your demographics are, what type of content they respond to and create a plan for that audience.

You may find a similar demographic listens to a particular radio station in town. Why not have an ad that talks to that audience. Having your online data cannot only help you make a more informed decision in this example, but it can also help you write that 30-second ad.

3) **More Personal**

Digital marketing is an ideal way to reach out to a specific audience, while traditional marketing is an effective way of reaching a broad customer base. Using both marketing techniques will allow you to build relationships with clients that are more relevant and deeper.

Look to personalize your digital marketing campaigns with geo-targeting features on your website or in email campaigns. Some features not only allow you to target by broad location but also IP address and Name.

Thus, it is highly important that you combine both traditional and digital marketing techniques to improve the performance and offline authority of your firm. In the next chapter, we will discuss how you can use digital marketing techniques to build your online authority for your law firm.

Where Do I Start?

Budget, budget, budget. If you are just starting out, I would not necessarily suggest allocating a large portion of your budget to radio, television, or billboards. If you can afford to do so, by all means, get started. Otherwise, set up a strategy that allows you to hand out those business cards or brochures. Find networking events in town that fit your profile.

In large cities, this is fairly easy as there are events daily. You just have to know where to find them. Just remember, you are not at these events to sell everyone on your services. Build your profile at these events first, and it will pay off over time.

Also, remember that your traditional marketing should tie into your online strategy in some fashion. Recording a radio spot? Great! In the end, we typically hear a phone number to reach your firm 24/7 correct? Why not add in your website at the end?

Your ad could look like this, "Call XYZ Law Firm Today at XXX-XXXX or reach us online at www.yourlawfirm.com/ESPN."

Do see what I did there at the end? This is under the assumption that your ad is for the local ESPN radio station. Why not add the ESPN URL to your site as a landing page that you can track? Do this with all of your traditional marketing.

Not everyone will call, but those that may not call could go to your website. You have to direct your audience to what action you want them to take in both traditional and online marketing. Do not assume that they can just find you online. Tell them where they can go for more information and track everything.

Chapter 4 – A Look at Digital Marketing and Your Law Firm

Digital marketing refers to advertising via digital channels, such as mobile apps, email, social media, search engines and websites. While the term covers a wide range of marketing activities, all of which are not universally agreed upon, we will look at a few areas that make up digital marketing.

Local SEO

Local SEO is one of the most effective methods of digital marketing. It helps you promote your services to potential client in your local area at the exact time they are looking for them. Over the last few years, Local SEO has grown rapidly due to increased Smartphone usage and better connectivity.

So, why is local SEO important? First, local customers are turning to the internet to find local businesses on their desktop and mobile phones. Research shows that 96 percent of PC owners do local searches when they need a product or service and a whopping 78 percent of local mobile searches result in an offline purchase.

Secondly, mobile search is growing. More and more consumers use tablets or phones to find local business while they are on the move. In fact, time spent on mobile phones in the United States is now higher than 51 percent compared to desktop use at 42 percent. If utilized properly, Local SEO covers both mobile and PC internet access meaning you will never miss out a potential client.

How do you improve your Local SEO? There are many tips and suggestions to improve local SEO in Quick Time. Here are 9 valuable tips:

1. Claim and verify your Google My Business Listing
2. Build local links consistently and responsibly
3. Respond to all directory reviews
4. Optimize your onsite content to be geo-targeted
5. Add Local Business and Review schema to your site
6. Implement a strategy to get reviews across multiple directories
7. Remove duplicate listings on the directories that matter for your clients
8. Optimize your citations
9. Ensure your NAP citations are consistent across the directories that matter most for your firm

Local SEO trends are strong now, and they are going to get stronger and more significant in the future. Keep in mind that Google has over 200 ranking factors.

Website Design and Structure for UX

Site structure refers to how your website is set up, that is, how the individual subpages are linked to one another. It is particularly important that Google and Bing find all subpages easily and quickly. A great site structure will help you rank high in search engines.

In addition to that, site structure is also important for the user experience (UX). If your site structure is clear your target audience will easily find their way on your website. A good UX will increase the odds of your targets converting to subscribe to your newsletter, hire your services or return for another visit. UX cannot be understated. With recent changes over the years, Google is starting to become more transparent in their goal to provide potential users with the content they are searching for. Relevancy comes in to play here.

If your content is about you and your law firm, guess what? You have provided little to no value for your potential clients in the eyes of Google, and you will be penalized with lower rankings over time.

This is a welcome change from the wild west times of setting up a site and keyword stuffing until you reach number one. This should also bring to light the need for goal setting in your overall marketing strategy. What are you trying to accomplish? I have said it once, and I will say it again, an inbound phone call should be priority number one for a law firm.

With all that said, developing a good site can be overwhelming. There are few things you can do to create a strong site structure. First, plan your sitemap or site hierarchy before developing your website. Ensure your sitemap is SEO friendly and will make sense to your target audience.

Secondly, determine what kind of content you will include on your website and how it will be categorized to make sense to your users. Third, ensure users who are first being introduced to your firm will easily be able to locate the content they are looking for. Your site hierarchy should be simple and make sense to you and your target audience.

Lastly, ensure that the site structure you are developing is simple. Avoid using a navigation system that overly complicated. Use as few steps as possible for a user to find the content they are looking for. More importantly, make sure that the main content categories are located in your site header at the top of your main navigation menu.

Remember, the user experience is a priority right now, and it does not look like Google is going to reverse this focus. You might as well get used to it and plan accordingly.

Link Building

Link building is the process of acquiring hyperlinks from other sites to your website. In the world of SEO, these types of links, also known as inbound links, external links or backlinks, are seen as a valuable endorsement for a site. They serve as a quality signal to search engines and can help in increasing a website's brand awareness and conversions as well as significantly impact a website's organic traffic.

Link building can be done in many ways:

- Guest blogging
- Use of infographics
- Following blog comments
- Following social bookmarking websites
- Submission to article directories (careful here, we will address in citations)
- Writing pillar content and informing bloggers

Keep in mind that not all links are created equal. This goes in line with keyword stuffing. Things have changed. I have created sites for clients that rank #1 in the Google 3-pack with less than 50 links. These sites have outranked their competitors that had well over 1000 links. It is about quality, not quantity.

Look at the bullets above again. Although I have the submission to directories listed, I would never tell you to spam as many directories as possible. There are some directories that took major hits after Google algorithm updates and can do your site more harm than good. Do your research first and then use some common sense.

Again, I say this because I have seen it. Do you really think your Family Law website belongs in a directory of out of state plumbers for the sake of getting a link? Probably not. Guess what, Google knows that also. At the same time, should your law firm be listed in a local business directory?

Schema/ Markup

Schema markup is a micro-data or code that you put on your site to help search engines provide more useful and relevant results to the users. This micro-data may include hints that help search engines interpret and categorize that you want to highlight, and then present it in rich snippet form. Schema markups allow your law firm to share a more immediate path to information users are looking for and increase search engine rankings at the same time.

Schema does not impact how your site is crawled. However, it changes the way your site displays information. Instead of just telling search engines what your web page is about, a schema markup will assign meaning to your content.

Using schema, search engines can identify and display snippets of information that your target audience may be looking for, such as contact info, business hours and even payment types. Additionally, it can be used to apply markup to phrases or words that have different meanings in various texts. This code is not visible at all to users unless they look at your source code.

For the life of me, I am not sure why I do not see more law firms utilizing Schema, and I believe that it may be out of fear of the unknown. This has been one of the first items I cover for clients and their sites, and it brings them fast results in search. You can use the Structured Data tools provided by Google Search Console to mark up your site page by page. There are also various plugins in WordPress that assist in marking up websites.

If you are not using Schema, I highly suggest you get started because a few of your competitors are a couple of years ahead of you.

AMP (Accelerated Mobile Pages)

Accelerated Mobile Pages (AMP) are created to improve speed and user experience, across all platforms and devices, by cutting down on many of the components that lead to a slow web page. To increase site speed, AMP strips down caches content and HTML pages to Google servers and then serve the content from there.

Google also pre-renders Accelerated Mobile Pages in SERPs before users visit them, allow for near-instant loading time. AMP makes use of a smart-resource downloading, to be able to download content from your website and transfers it Google's viewport for better viewing. In addition, AMP uses other numerous components to enhance the interactivity of AMP pages, such as amp-lightbox and amp-iframe.

These components can also include CTA boxes or banners coded to your AMP profile specifically. There are features being added constantly within AMP to improve the look and feel of your mobile site. GitHub is a great resource if you are doing this in house. If you are outsourcing your marketing, you need to ask about the marketing firms ability to create and implement AMP with the features you need to convert potential clients into phone calls for your law firm.

Google announced some time ago that there would be a focus on mobile first. Well, it is here, and AMP is must have for your law firm if you want to compete. Just like Schema, I have not seen firms utilize this feature enough. I am sure that will change soon as early adopters in the legal profession are already a step ahead.

PPC

PPC stands for Pay Per Click, it is a form of digital advertising in which advertisers display ads for their goods or service, and when users click on these ads, the advertiser pays a fee. Essentially, it is a method of buying customer visits to your site instead of waiting for organic visits.

Google AdWords is one of the mostly used PPC ad words platforms. This platform allows you to create ads that are shown on search engines and other Google Platforms.

A PPC campaign is based on selected keywords. To get the best out of your PPC campaign, you should refine and grow your keyword list continuously. A good PPC keyword list should be expansive, exhaustive and relevant.

After creating your new PPC campaign, you need to manage them regularly to ensure they continue being effective. One of the ways of optimizing your campaigns is by adding negative keywords. Adding non-converting terms, as negative keywords can improve campaign relevancy and reduce wasted spend. Other adjustments you can make to optimize your campaigns include splitting Ad groups, adding search keywords, refining landing pages and reviewing costly PPC keywords.

I have seen campaigns drop over 80% in Cost-per-click. Although that makes us look good, my question is, "What in the hell were you doing before?" If I can see an 80% drop in cost-per-click, someone was not managing your account very well to begin with. I am not complaining, but I say that to point out this.

Ask questions. You may be reading this book to get an overview and increase your knowledge base, and that is exactly the purpose. You are an attorney, not a marketer, but you have to know enough to ask questions and challenge your marketing team, whether in-house or outsourced, to be more efficient with your money.

PPC can generate a ton of inbound calls and income for your firm; it can also become a huge waste of money if not managed properly.

Where Do I Start?

If you have a site up and running, I would suggest starting with Google AdWords…but only if you have content. Here is why. The biggest gains I have seen in AdWords campaigns come when the potential clients go to a page that provides the content they are searching for. You have seen me mention UX or user experience often. There is a reason for that. It is called Google.

One of the basis points for creating their ad Quality Score is the user experience. Just as in mobile and search, the same happens in their paid advertising. The reasoning is that if the potential client clicks on your ad and the ad either answers their question or provides them information related to their question, then they had a positive experience on your website. This, in turn, lowers your cost-per-click.

Now let's take a step back. My first sentence was, "If you have a site up and running…"

If you have an active site that has blog content, get into your Google Analytics and see which content is the most popular from an SEO standpoint. If you already see positive activity, then go to AdWords and write your campaigns to the questions that are being answered in your current content, direct users to those pages, and clarify your call to action.

You can also jump into AdWords and create "Call Only" ads. These ads are specifically for mobile users with a goal of calling you directly without going to your website. These ads do convert as long as your ad is speaking to what your potential client is searching for.

With any of your AdWords campaigns, make sure you are often monitoring as mismanagement can lead to a waste of your hard-earned money.

Chapter 5: Building Your Online Reputation

Online reputation and your potential clients' perception of your firm go hand-in-hand. I can remember one client in particular that had a website well over 15 years old. The site looked old. It looked low-end. I am not a fan of having a pretty website for show, but I am a proponent of putting your best foot forward online. To show this to the ownership team, we did a walk-in survey for a week and asked clients what they thought of the website.

Sure enough, clients thought the site looked old and low-end. This online reputation did not match the firm by any means. Their office was very much high-end, bright, and energetic. You may read that and say, "So what does that matter." It matters a lot to your potential clients.

Think of it this way. Would you want your clients walking into a sloppy lobby or office space? If your answer is no, then you should look at your online reputation in the same manner. Start with your website and then move on to other areas that create the perception and reputation of your firm online.

Here are 7 tips to help you build a positive online reputation.

Tip 1: Be Active on Social Media
Today, your potential clients are on social media. It is the best relationship and trust building platform, and they are checking you out. You need to develop a comprehensive social media

strategy to help you manage your online reputation. It is also important that you use the right social media platforms while engaging with your potential clients. Regardless of the social media platform you choose to use, following these four rules will help your social media strategy to succeed.

- **Be Aware & Share:** Take time to listen to the conversation happening via social media about your industry, you will be amazed at the insights you will get. Share your professional opinion and industry knowledge as appropriate to the platform and your audience.

- **Be Meaningful:** Always publish content that is meaningful and useful to your target audience. Establish yourself and your firm as the go-to source for information meaningful to your target audience.

- **Be Authentic:** Just as in any walk of life, try your best not to come off as fake. Once you dive into social media, your personality will eventually show up in how you post and respond. Your desire to be a trusted resource must come off as authentic to potential clients.

- **Be Focused:** Once you create a goal for a specific platform, stick to it. It is essential to define your goal and focus the majority of your social media activity on that area. Try to understand your target audience and what interests them by taking into account their interests, behavior, and demographics.

When using social media to build an online reputation, you must ensure you choose the right platforms. Some of the most popular social media platforms include Twitter, Facebook, and LinkedIn. However, it is essential to consider which social networks your potential clients are accessing and start out with them. Once you have chosen your platforms, post unique and interesting content for your target audience.

Try positing interesting and entertaining videos, blog post, photos or curate content from other experts in the field. Using social media is an ideal way of building your online reputation, engaging with prospective and current clients and building your law firm's credibility.

Tip 2: Reviews and Testimonials Are Vital
Feedback is valuable. It shows you who is interacting with you and gives you a significant insight into your reputation. Reviews should be welcomed with open-arms, as about 90 percent of review readers believe what they read online, according to a recent study. Always check and maintain your profiles on various review sites.

Even if you get negative reviews about your firm, reply professionally with a solution or an apology. Ignoring negative reviews will help your audience believe the reviewer. With the help of RSS readers, Google Alert and related reputation management services, get updates on the reviews about your firm on various social media platforms, review sites, and blog sites.

It is not always necessary that you receive a positive review because you cannot satisfy everyone on earth. However, you can request your happy clients to post positive reviews about your firm. Request them to share their great experience with the world and help your customers understand how motivating it is to hear good words from them. More importantly, display customer testimonials on your site.

When possible, display third-party reviews, such as those on Facebook, Avvo, Google, or Yelp.

As a marketer, I would suggest not avoiding the power of reviews in your marketing strategy, specifically with Google. Having positive reviews on your Google Maps listing will not only assist in building your online reputation, but they have the bonus of improving your 3-pack ranking.

If your website is on a WordPress platform, keep in mind that you can place reviews from Facebook and Google directly on your website. Not to get too technical, but the way the code is written for both, the plugins allow the reviews to be crawled by Google.

Tip 3: Communicate Through Your Blog

A blog is a great vehicle that helps you give credible information your firm as well attract potential clients with useful observations and tips. You can establish yourself as a legal expert which gives your law firm greater credibility. Blogging helps you to build a strong relationship with your target audience.

Start your blog, as about 81 percent of people read and trust blogs. Blogging also helps you to deal with misconceptions and rumors about your firm. They give you space to discuss your services in detail and allow your target audience to know how you are better than your competitors.

I am going to back up a second here. I mentioned that blogging deals with misconceptions and rumors about your firm. That sounds petty and childish, right? Well, guess what, competition brings out the worst in some people. Do not, and I repeat DO NOT, get into a reputation campaign contest against a competitor on your blog.

If you are reading that asking why I would even mention it here, it is because I have seen it in action. It will not end well for your firm.

Also, remember that your content needs to be client-centered. A well-written blog will build your reputation and show off your authority to your potential clients and competitors.

Tip 4: Build Your Content Repository

Apart from posting content on your site, social media pages, and blogs as well as dealing with reviews, you need to build your firm's content repository by leveraging your relationship with other influential platforms. Let's understand this with an example.

Suppose there is a webinar on types of personal injury case, and you work as a personal injury attorney. It is important to participate in such a webinar and give credible info or solutions to allow people to know your knowledge and experience levels. Additionally, you should do guest blogging or hire an internet marketing firm to have your blogs posted on relevant websites with high view results in your niche.

Tip 5: Have a Client Case Portfolio and Always Be Transparent

Build a comprehensive case portfolio that showcases a list of your satisfied clients and what you have done for them. This portfolio needs to be relevant and preferably up-to-date. Showing cases from five years ago are not as impactful as an updated portfolio monthly or quarterly.

Clients want to know that you are actively working. I know, it may sound silly to say that, but it is true. Just because you have a website up and you show on up in Google, does not necessarily mean you are a successful law firm. I have seen this in other industries as well. The website goes up, and the owner assumes that people will show up. Not true.

You are not a cell phone shop that can just throw up a website and let it go. Even if you were a cell phone shop, I would advise against being apathetic when it comes to building your reputation as the number one source of information in the area.

Having a portfolio that speaks to your consistency of winning for your clients goes a long way in building your reputation online.

Tip 6: Get a Local Citation
A local citation allows you to mention your law firm over the internet on popular law websites or those in your locality. It includes the name of your law firm, phone number and complete address. It is essential for you to have the same citation details on every website for Google and your audience.

If you are reading this thinking it sounds similar to link building, you are correct. Remember that we are looking to place these citations on trusted local and industry websites. You have to perform some due diligence before your submission though.

Make sure that your website will not show on sites that you will not approve of such as sites with adult content, etc. Although you may have some potential clients visiting those sites, do you want the reputation of your site to be so closely associated?

Tip 7: Always Offer Quality Services
Last but not least, you are done with half of the job, but the next half fully depends on the client service you offer. You need to

please your clients with what you have promised to offer to the best of your ability. Their first-hand experience is what will lead to word of mouth marketing and help your law firm grow exponentially.

You would not believe some of the calls I have listened to over the years. Almost every client that I have worked with believes that their customer or client service is outstanding from the first phone call through the end of the case. I challenge you to listen to a month of phone calls from your team. You may learn some things about why you have so many missed appointments or clients are simply not retaining you.

Some of you are losing clients because your first impression on the phone does not match the reputation you have built online. I could go over story after story of clients turning away or completely turning off potential new business because the staff is rude, unprepared, or lack knowledge of what the firm can handle regarding of types of cases.

In no way do I believe most front office staff is doing this on purpose. Being a former sales manager though, I can tell you that if you are not inspecting what you expect, you may never know.

Remember, getting inbound calls is the purpose of your marketing. That is why you spend the money or put the time and effort into creating your brand and marketing message. If your data is showing that you are getting a good number of phone calls, but not getting a sufficient amount of appointments, then it is time to start listening to your calls.

If you are questioning how a phone call plays into your online reputation, imagine this. A potential client calls your team after reading a well-written article about how your strategy has solved (insert problem). Your team gets the call, and for whatever reason, your front office staff is short and comes off as unprofessional. Maybe they were in the middle of something else, who knows? Would you?

Since your law firm is listed on Google, you are going to get an email with the header, "You just received an online review." You open the email, and this potential client, whom you have not even had the chance to talk to says, "Staff was rude, would not recommend using this firm. Sounds like they are all about the money."

That is an actual review, verbatim, from a client. They had zero idea who the person was but at this point, the damage is done. Can you overcome this? Sure you can. Jump on, respond immediately and have the client call you directly. This will show others that you care about your online reputation and are willing to reach out when you see both positive and negative reviews.

The real question is, should you have to in the first place? Bottom line, inspect what you expect when it comes to your reputation. Marketing is not done until the phone call gets the potential client in your office and your staff is an extension of you and your law firms reputation.

Now that you understand the importance of online reviews and building a good online reputation follow the 7 expert-proven tips to make your law firm reach new heights. Take your negative reviews as feedback and work towards betterment. To grow your firm, you need to build a chain to trust and quality, and this chain will grow with your good online reputation.

Where Do I Start?

First, go and claim or create your business listings on these sites:

- Facebook
- Twitter
- Foursquare
- LinkedIn
- AVVO
- Yelp
- FindLaw
- Google My Business
- Bing Local Business (also creates Yahoo)

Anywhere that your potential clients can leave a review, get there and claim it. This will also help in creating citations for your website. Speaking of citations, be careful of the sites that you want to submit your RSS Feed or Guest Post blog content.

Not all sites are created equal in this regard. Google repeatedly cracks down on garbage across the web and your citations being on sites Google considers spam will have a negative impact on your online reputation.

Next, sit down with your team and come up with a strategy to address NEGATIVE comments and reviews. Anyone can respond to positive reviews but having a strategy for the negative reviews is more important in my opinion. Here is why.

Your law firm is your baby, and you will protect it at all costs. There are times when your first reaction to a negative review is not always the best reaction. Having a plan in place to consistently handle negative reviews will take some of your initial emotion out of your response.

Also, make sure you have the app for these sites downloaded to your phone or an office managers phone. Nothing worse than seeing a review that is a month old that you did not know about. Your response time goes directly to the online reputation of your firm. Let your potential clients know that you are engaged and paying attention to what they are saying, both positive and negative.

Chapter 6: Call Tracking and Conversation Analytics

What is Call Tracking?

Call tracking is just as it sounds. The ability to track calls that are the result of marketing efforts. Although this may appear to be something that is new to marketing, it is anything but new. Have you heard of the Yellow Pages? That is right, the old Yellow Page.

You essentially tracked your marketing efforts by the calls associated with certain ads. Those ads could be in the newspaper, billboards, on the side of the bus or wherever old-school ad agencies offered to place your brand.

So is this new, not at all. It is however interesting that some law firms are finally seeing the value to using these numbers for digital marketing efforts over the last few years. Are there technical issues that arise from call tracking? There could be if implemented incorrectly.

For instance, NAP (Name, Address, Phone #) could impact your SEO if done incorrectly. For the most part, however, the marketers that I have worked with and run across understand how to properly implement the correct code in order not to impact your search presence.

With that said, there is an area that most marketers and law firms are missing out on. That area is in Conversation Analytics.

What is Conversation Analytics?

Conversation Analytics digs deeper into the calls generated from marketing. If used properly, the analytics taken from your call tracking numbers can help improve your marketing focus by providing long-tail keywords that your potential clients are looking for.

With the right call tracking system, you should be able to transcribe each call that comes in through various marketing channels. Once you have these transcriptions, you can run reports in your system to identify common occurrences of keywords. This will be tedious at first as you have zero data to work with. Over time, it will get easier, and you will be able to take those keywords and write content that your audience is telling you they are looking for.

Why is this going to be important? Google and Bing say so that is why. Natural language search is already being utilized and tracked on Google. If you have an AdWords account, you know this already. Go into your account and look in the "search terms" section. You may find some keywords that look like sentences. These are most likely from mobile users. From your AdWords back office and your call tracking system, you should be able to cross-reference and see the similarities. Take this information and start writing your paid ads and your content to match.

Conversation Analytics for Training

Here is where having a background as a sales leader comes in to play. For the years that I led inside sales teams, we utilized conversation analytics as a training tool for our teams to improve performance. We also used it as a training and communication tool for other sales leaders on how to properly coach and train their teams to increase overall performance.

I would be able to pull up calls from employees at any given time and listen to things such as:

- Phone Presence
- Product Knowledge
- Compliance
- Call Flow
- Hold Times
- Customer Service

Now let's look at that bulleted list again. Is your firm utilizing your call tracking software to its maximum capability? Would you know how to utilize your current systems? Do you even have access to your call tracking system provided by your marketing team?

If used correctly and to its full potential, your call tracking software should provide more than just basic marketing data.

The Law

No matter the industry, there are core areas that must be addressed when listening to your team's calls.

First things first, know the law. There are some states that require you to notify the one or both parties that calls are being recorded. There are 12 states specifically that require informing all parties (Journalistresource.org, 2012). For an updated list, I suggest going Journalistresource.org and reading their legal guide to phone conversations.

To be on the safe side, your call system should have what we call a "whisper" feature to inform both parties that a call is not only inbound but that the call is being recorded for training purposes. I know telling a lawyer to "be on the safe side" provides little assurance, but here is the more practical reason.

Who is to say that you will not have an out-of-state caller? I have clients that received calls from clients in other countries and multiple states. You cannot assume that all of your potential calls will come from within your state only.

Call Structure Fundamentals

When talking fundamentals of the calls themselves, I never have and will never suggest reading from a script. I have trained in the flooring, financial service, retail, education, and legal field.

In each industry, I have heard the "script" version of a call, and all of them are crap. Yes, there is a flow to a call and things we must hit to deem a call successful, but please, whatever you do, let's not have your team sounding like robots.

Instead, put up an outline or bullets of things to hit during an initial conversation. Here's an example:

- Intro
- Repeat Clients Name
- Ask for Call Back Number
- Which type of Case do they require assistance?
- Repeat type of case for clarification
- Confirm Next Step

This is not an encompassing list, nor is it the detail of a call flow, but it should be a starting point. This goes back to goal setting and the ability to train to reach your goals.

If you can identify bottlenecks in the phone conversion process, then this will go a long way in increasing your set appointment rates. You will also get the most value out of your call tracking software.

Conversation Analytics Outside the Box

Strategic Partnerships

By now, you may have a better understanding of the importance of tracking our marketing data and training our staffs with analytics, but what else can we do?

When using conversation analytics correctly, your law firm could find a few additional benefits if we thought outside the box:

- Create new revenue streams

- Deliver an improved customer experience

How can we create a win-win-win for all involved? Let's look at one of the many scenarios that could arise.

The Scenario

Let's say that we own a successful law practice. Our firm concentrates in DUI, Personal Injury, and Family Law. Over the past year or so, we notice that our Family Law portion of the practice may not fit with our model moving forward, so we decide to walk away and focus on DUI and Personal Injury.

We are happy with our decision over the next few months, but by using conversation analytics properly, we notice that we are still receiving calls for Family Law and turning away clients. Keep in mind; we have spent a considerable amount of money over the years on marketing our firm with all three specialties.

After a deeper look into our call data, we discover that we have a choice to make:

- Keep turning "bad leads" away, thus wasting a portion of our marketing budget

- Form a strategic partnership with a Family Law practice

After looking at the data, we decide on Number 2.

We identify three firms that specialize in Family Law and in no way cross-over into our specialties of DUI and Personal Injury.

We decide on a young lawyer just starting out, like we once were, and see that her firm could make the most sense for both parties. After some discussion with this particular lawyer, we find that another decision needs to be made:

1. Do we charge her firm for our leads or,

2. We decide to trade leads

We decided that since her firm does not have the proper tools in place to provide us enough data to make us comfortable choosing Number 2, we decide on Number 1. We are going to charge her firm $5 per lead (for illustration purposes only).

We are ready to go now. Our reporting data is set, and we have our system in place to track and distribute leads, and we are also going to take it step further.

We are going to warm transfer the calls over to our partner of choice, simply because we pride ourselves on above and beyond customer service.

Possible Outcomes

So we have made our decision, and our system is in place. After a few months of using conversation analytics to track our internal data, gaining feedback through NPS (Net Promoter Scores) and other resources in place to gain feedback, from both our partner and clients, we have created the following:

- A level of customer service that gives a potential client a memorable "wow" experience. Who knows, they may need your firm later.

- Goodwill with our strategic partner. In this instance, we are helping out a fellow lawyer whom one day wants a practice as successful as yours, but she may need a little help getting off the ground.

- If we are selling these leads to our partner, at a reasonable price point for both parties, we still gain a benefit from our past marketing efforts and budget.

What type of partnerships could your firm develop?

Would this be guess work today, or do you have the data to support making such a decision?

Would this type of partnership benefit you? It may or may not, but again, start thinking outside of the box, and there may be other unexpected benefits available to you and your firm.

Where Do I Start?

You have to pick the right system that matches the goals of your firm. I will always believe in call tracking because as a marketer, it is a trackable way for me to show value.

There are a few companies out there that can provide call tracking for your marketing if you are either a small law firm or doing this in-house. The systems are pretty straight forward. I would recommend looking at one these two options but keep in mind; there are others on the market:

- Call Rail
- Call Tracking Metrics

I have utilized both for myself and clients. Jump on one of their webinars so that you can see what each brings to the table. The other option is to build your own system. Keep in mind that your costs for development will not be cheap on your wallet or time. If you want to go that route, check out GitHub. There are developers on GitHub that will point you in the right direction.

Chapter 7: Creating Closed-Loop Analytics to Improve Conversions

There are two questions that you should ask yourself about your marketing campaigns.

1. Do you know where your clients are coming from?
2. Can you easily calculate the ROI of your campaigns?

If you cannot answer these questions, you certainly should figure out the answers and stop wasting your money.

What's Our Marketing ROI?

Research shows that 77 percent of business managers believe that marketing teams are focused on the wrong things. Their perception is that, rather than tracking ROI and revenue, marketers are more focused on things like value and brand equity. It is certainly not a flattering perception. Perhaps, a complete lack of ROI tracking is shameful in a world where access to user-friendly technology is abundant.

There is a shift in the marketing profession towards creating added value by proving ROI within the entire marketing cycle. In my opinion, the best marketers are already at this point and can show their value to the penny instead of "educated" guessing.

In working with law firms, I am surprised that more firms are not requiring more data, but after working with attorneys and leaders in other industries, it makes sense. I believe that some marketers are uncomfortable with providing that data. Especially to attorneys.

Attorneys, by nature, ask questions and do their best to find a proper solution that fits their client's problem. The same should be done with marketing for attorneys. The example I used earlier was that attorneys are not selling widgets like other local businesses. Since we know this to be true, why is your marketing strategy the same as the local repair shop? Why is your reporting data the same? What is your goal?

For a repair shop let's say the goal is to generate walk-in business. Having done marketing work in that industry, I can tell you that repair shops seldom get phone calls. Reviews are huge in that industry, so the repair shop needs to rank in the Google 3-pack, have an active social media following, and their blogs can talk about local events, cell phone features, new apps for kids, etc.

Does that sound like the two of you should have the same strategy? Sure there are things that cross over between the two but the goals are not the same. The same goes for tracking what data is most important to you and your law firm.

To track your entire marketing process and cycle properly, you should look at implementing closed-loop analytics.

So, What Exactly Is Closed-Loop Analytics?

Also known as closed-loop marketing, closed-loop analytics opens lines of communication between your front desk, marketing department and leadership. It allows you to know how clients found your law firm. It traces their journey from the first time they visited your site to their final conversion, sitting down in your office.

Closed-loop analytics is a process of gathering massive amounts of data into easy-to-consume reports that profile your clients and their journey. It provides marketers with a better look on how customers will respond to their campaigns. For this type of system to work, the right systems must be in place.

This would mean that we should also not forget the value of conversation analytics in your marketing analytics as well. In listening to calls, not only will you see the journey your clients took to the phone, you may also pick up data within the call. Creating and utilizing a closed-loop analytics report will help your law firm capture valuable data that can be used for your decision-making when it comes to marketing budgets and messaging.

Closed-loop analytics has four major stages that focus on the customer's journey through the sales funnel. These steps are discussed below:

1. **Attraction: The Visitors Get to Your Website**
   With the help of cookies and other tools, it is easy to tell what brought a visitor to your website. Whether they were on Facebook or Twitter and found a very attractive post from your firm, searching for a specific term or checking

their emails for the latest news and updates. Determining what brought them will help you know which marketing methods are working best for your firm.

2. **Interest: The Visitor Browses around Your Website**
   What keeps the visitor on your site? As you track your visitor's behavior while they are on your website, you will learn more about what interests them most, which pages they like most and those that cause them to click away.

   To know and track your visitor behavior, you are going to have to expand your tool box and knowledge base. There are numerous tools you can utilize. Google Analytics can drill down to site behavior, exit pages and more. Using these features will show you entry and exit points along your visitor's journey. Add the use of heat maps to enhance your view of visitor behavior as well.

3. **Conversion: Visitor Converts into a Lead**
   This is the most important stage in the process from a marketing standpoint. Once we understand what actions were taken to turn visitors into leads, we can then replicate this process.

   Keep this in mind. You are an attorney, and your market is very competitive. Do not fool yourself into thinking you are the only attorney this potential client is contacting. Since that is the case, you must make the process of becoming a lead easy for your potential clients, but there is another piece that most law firms are missing. You have to be first to contact.

If a visitor fills out a contact form and it takes you 24-48 hours to contact them, you have just wasted your money on marketing in my opinion. Your mobile site must have a "call now" feature. To take this a step further, you also need to look at your contact form. If you are utilizing call tracking, you can make your form "auto call" your visitor and your office, simultaneously, within seconds after the form is filled out.

Why do this? First off, it is one of those "wow" factors for potential clients. I have listened to hundreds of inbound calls when implementing this feature for clients. Potential clients love it, and they say so during initial contact. Second, why give your client a chance to look anywhere else. Again, this is where you differ from other industries, and your lead conversion strategy needs to differ from your competitors.

4. **Retention: Lead Becomes an Appointment**
This is where your front office staff and telephone conversion analytics comes into the equation. With the right call tracking system set up, your staff can assist your marketing efforts by asking the proper probing questions to set an appointment.

If done correctly, these probing questions can be taken directly from your analytics and transferred into content, branding, and messaging across whichever platform they found your firm.

The right call tracking system will also allow you to inspect what you expect regarding phone handling of your hard earned leads. I have heard the missed appointment from a staff member that is not confident or lacks the proper knowledge of the firm's operations on the phone. Worse yet, I have heard it from junior attorneys who happen to be covering the front desk.

There is a ton of information that call tracking can bring to your marketing campaigns that go beyond simple sourcing. To win in your competitive market, you are going to need all of the analytics you can get your hands on to make better decisions in marketing and conversion.

Closed-loop analytics and a sound conversion strategy enable you to set better goals, reduce your conversion cycle and gain important insights on your client's personas. Implement this model with your team today to discover just how profitable integration between marketing and conversion can be.
Let's take a look at some other points to made regarding Closed-loop Analytics.

Now that you understand the importance of closed-loop analytics, how do you use it to improve marketing and conversions? In practice, closed-loop analytics involves comparing data between two or more analytic tools. In most cases, marketers track their campaigns using tools such as Google Analytics.

Similarly, your front desk or operations manager tracks leads with help of CRM software. To get a full view of the customers' life cycle, closed-loop marketing requires that the person measuring metrics review tracking platforms used by both the front office staff and marketing departments. Here is a basic look at how you can use closed-loop marketing to improve your ROI Analysis

Improved ROI Analysis

Marketers should always be tracking customer referral sourcing and drilling down the ROI of each marketing campaign they launch. Using a closed-loop analytics tool helps you to determine the social media channels, forms of content marketing and emails lead nurturing campaigns that provide the best results. Analyzing these numbers manually would be an exhaustive task.

How to Use Closed-Loop Analytics to Increase Conversions

Closed-loop analytics allows you to know and understand not only which channels drive traffic, but also which channels bring visitors who are likely to convert to customers. Closed-loop analytics will help to continually refine and adjust your visitor's personas. Rather than basing your client's profiles off a few interviews, you will be able to apply insights from your website visitor base to your marketing both online and offline.

Increased Conversion Rates

Closed-loop analytics help your firm to transform anonymous web visitors into identifiable prospective clients that can be converted into clients. It offers a holistic view of your complete marketing and sales process allowing you to determine what channels and tactics are actually leading to leads, conversions, and sales.

How to Use Closed-Loop Analytics to Improve Your Marketing

Even though marketing is part of intuition and creativity, your marketing department must still use and show hard facts and results, especially when it is time to report to the firm's executive suite. Closed-loop analytic tools, such as HubSpot which can integrate blogging, content management, social media, email marketing and automated lead nurturing into a single tool, provide valuable data about the performance of individual marketing tactics.

This allows marketers to determine what marketing tactics are working for the firm. This way they can choose to invest more in these tactics to improve the firm's performance based on data.

Reduced Marketing Costs

Even though firms as a whole benefit from using closed-loop analytics, marketers in particular stand to gain the most from this practice. This is because it allows them to know what marketing methods and tactics are working for the firm. This consequently helps the firm to reduce its marketing costs, by only investing in those methods that demonstrate true value to company.

Lastly, closed-loop analytics will allow you to see some real weaknesses in your marketing strategies. What social media posts and workflows fail to lead to paying clients? These should be carefully assessed and improved. Closed-loop analytics allows you to know what is working and where you need serious improvements to increase conversion.

Analyzing marketing efforts is vital for refining strategies so that they produce the greatest return on investment. Using timely, insightful closed-loop analytics allows your law firm to quickly prune away unproductive marketing techniques and replace them with strategies that engage target markets well and lead to increased conversion.

Appendix

These questionnaires are not an exhaustive list of questions to ask. Let these two checklists serve as a starting point for your law firm.

In-house Marketing Questionnaire

Branding

Does your brand clearly communicate what services your law firm can deliver?

Does your brand effectively differentiate you from every other attorney in the area?

Is your brand promise well understood and consistently executed at all levels of the law firm?

Is your brand identity being properly used in all media content?

Marketing

Can your potential clients afford your services? Are you willing to create payment options if necessary?

Can you identify you the top four (4) factors that your potential clients consider when selecting your law firm's representation in each vertical? Are your marketing campaigns focused on those factors?

Can you identify how your potential clients find your law firm online and offline? Have you adjusted your marketing plan accordingly?

Messaging

Do you have three to five key marketing messages that you're consistently delivering in all media?

Do your marketing messages resonate with your potential clients in each vertical?

Do these messages match the experience customers have when they interact with your staff?

Are you 100% certain that all of your staff knows the types of cases you can and cannot cover? When is the last time you checked?

Are you tailoring messages to specific market segments when you have the opportunity to do so?

Marketing Channels

Are traditional marketing channels – such as advertising, direct marketing, and public relations – still delivering enough value to warrant the investment they require? What is the current monthly investment?

How are you currently utilizing your digital marketing channels?

Is it time to shift some – or more – of your marketing to new channels such as social media and mobile marketing?

Are you maximizing the value of the proprietary channels you control, such as newsletters, invoices, vehicles, and buildings?

Marketing Tactics

Do you know which marketing tactics are generating the best results at the lowest cost?

Can you cut the cost of any of your marketing activities by changing formats?

Are you integrating social media into traditional marketing tactics like direct mail and advertising?

Are you comfortable with using social media to market your law firm? Are you consistent? Are you compliant?

Are you utilizing Facebook Paid Ads, Google AdWords, or Bing Ads? If so, what is your current budget? Are you happy with your results?

What is your current ROI with your PPC campaigns?

Your Consultation Offer

Does your offer showcase your law firm, your attorneys or both?

Does your offer deliver real value to your potential clients?

Are you tailoring offers to specific potential clients in each vertical?

If your potential clients are filling out contact forms on your website, how long does it take to get in touch with your potential client to set a consultation?

Collateral and Engagement Tools

Are your brochures and displays accurate, complete, and up to date?

Is your firms marketing collateral integrated with your brand and your marketing campaigns?

Do you need new tools to educate prospects about the services your firm offers?

Data and Conversions

How do you define a lead in your marketing data?

What are your most important KPI's (Key Performance Indicators) in your marketing data?

Are you capturing current and potential client data to build a robust marketing database?

Are you compiling email addresses for an ongoing dialogue regarding your firm?

Are you tracking and recording response and transactional data to create full profiles of your customers and their behavior so you can target future marketing messages?

Are you tracking every NEW phone call into your law firm? How are you using this data?

Are you utilizing your telephone data to create processes and procedures to train your staff on phone handling protocol and etiquette?

Do you have all of your marketing data in one portal for instant access across your law firm?

Does your CRM (Client Relationship Management) system track your appointment setting conversion data?

What percentage of your potential clients have missed appointments? What system tracks this?

How often do you view your marketing and conversion data? Weekly, Monthly, Quarterly?

Website

Is your website client-centered, attorney-centered, or law firm-centered?

Is your site easy to navigate, with most information available in three clicks or less?

Is your site using AMP (Accelerated Mobile Pages)?

Are you delivering high-value content that establishes your credibility?

Are you inviting visitors to engage with you via blogs, podcasts, RSS feeds, and social media?

Is your site fully optimized for search engines?

Are you regularly adding new content and inbound links to increase your SEO rankings?

Who writes your content? Is this a team effort?

Is your website and content in compliance with your states ethics rules?

Reputation Management

How often do you ask for reviews?

Where are most of your reviews located? Google, Avvo, LinkedIn, Facebook?

Do your reviews have responses from your law firm directly to your clients? Are the responses professional?

Do you have a monthly target number of reviews?

Agency Questionnaire

How often will we have reporting data?

How often will we have a meeting regarding our data?

Will our internal team have login access to our data?

How often will our PPC campaign be managed? Will it be managed actively?

Are we charged a percentage of our ad buy? What is that percentage?

What is your SEO strategy? Will you focus on Local or Mobile first?

Do you use call tracking numbers?

Will those call tracking numbers impact our SEO?

Do you focus on our call conversions?

Will your staff or our staff grade our calls?

Do you offer staff training to improve our call conversion? If so, how much will that additional cost be monthly?

How will you handle our reputation management? Where will we focus the bulk of our reviews? Avvo, LinkedIn, Google, Facebook? Why?

How often will we be kept abreast of changes from Google and other search engine companies?

What will be our primary mode of communication?

How many hours will be dedicated to our law firms marketing efforts monthly?

Which social media platforms will our law firm be utilizing? Instagram, Twitter, Facebook, LinkedIn?

Do you have a separate strategy and target audience for each social media platform?

www.ingramcontent.com/pod-product-compliance
Lightning Source LLC
Chambersburg PA
CBHW071216220526
45468CB00002B/627